MOVE HIGHER IN YOUR PURPOSE

BEING YOUR BEST AT YOUR ONE BEST THING!

By: Nicole J. Christian & Edna J. White

Mind, Body, Spirit In Business (Trademark Pending/Copyright Protected,10/21/2015)

Foreword

How did we get here?

Both authors – Edna and I - both experienced traumatic physical and mental tragedy and triumph, me – major surgery and a divorce and Edna – sexual abuse and a near-fatal car accident. In 2008, we became reacquainted as sisters after over 10 years apart. We became the beginning of a large vibrant sisterhood of women entrepreneurs on Long Island. We were both religious and committed to traditional religious philosophy and like many others before us, life experience, soul ties and lessons from near death, allowed us to live an enhanced more encompassing spiritual consciousness that embraced not only our Judea- Christian origins, but the spiritual lessons of Tao, Buddhism, New Thought and the Feminine Divine. We are not heretics. We promote well-being, wholeness, joy, truth and clarity.

What do we want to share?

You are not a victim of fate. Your age does not limit you. Your weight does not limit you. Your bills and financial obligations do not limit you. Your spouse does not limit you. The church or religion does not limit you. Your children or child-freeness does not limit you. Set your own course. We desire to share with you our collective wisdom that has led to another level of living fully.

Use this Book and all the lessons. Including New Vocabulary.

When you read the guide, consider the suggestions and if you come to one of our "Creative Connect-ed Sessions" remember or record your impressions. Each day apply one new element of language. I have a close friend/family that inserts the word "whatever" and "this that and the other" into every empty space in her discussions, I suggested that she try to limit using those terms at least during one conversation a day. It takes time. I used to use word like "Do what you gotta do", "Whatever". "I don't care" and what I was doing was affirming those words about me to the universe. The Universe (God, Divine Wisdom, Beloved, All That is, etc.) provides what you affirm not what you ask for since what we ask for is often amiss. What we really need is what we affirm from our mouths. I only ask for what is beyond my power – and I do it as an affirmation. For example "My doctor gives me positive news about my exam". "My companion, life partner cherishes me and understands my humanness". Ask while affirming. There is no sin when your heart is pure and you truly believe.

What's inside?

Mind

- Perception
- Fear
- Ego
- Creativity Connectors

Body

- Choices
- The Pursuit of Happiness
- Health and Wealth?
- Where does the energy go?
- Helping vs. Sharing
- Make the Connection – the exercise

Spirit

- Questions from within
- Satisfied; being content is about more than having what you want
- Scaling down to build up
- Free

- Soul Ties

- Financial Bondage

- Symptoms of Bondage

- Remember

- The Connection – Nicole's Story

- Getting on Track

- Family: Victim or Villian

- Growing Spiritually

- Pay it forward

- Steps

- The Recession will not end in Y(our) lifetime

- Starting your own business in no longer just an option

- Ditch the "Work" Crowd

- Finally, choose love every time

Bonus

- Those affected by GFC 2007-10

This book is dedicated to all committed to staying in the light.

Should this book be a blessing to you and you want to share the word, go to your local library and request a copy to be purchased for your community.

Mind, Body, Spirit In Business (Trademark Pending/Copyright Protected,10/21/2015)

Mind

Embracing the concept and the depth of love for yourself is the most challenging and enriching exercise you can ever practice. There is so much in your life that you believe you could do better, more of, less of that love gets squeezed out. There just doesn't seem like there is enough time to look in the mirror and love every part, ounce, piece of who you are. This first chapter is completely about loving you. Not the same way you always have, but in a new way, a way that takes no prisoners and makes no mistakes. This love is perfect, blemish-less and pure. Remember how great you thought you were when you were 5 or 6 or maybe 18 or 20.

There was a time in every woman's life when she believed she was the cat's meow and that nothing would stop her. I remember a few instances in my life when I felt that love bubble up inside me: driving in the van with my mother when I left my home for college; when I graduated with my Master's; when I got married; when I played with my nieces in the backyard and laughed like there was no work tomorrow. Oh yes, you were great, in your own eyes and in your heart you never believed for a minute that you wouldn't have what you wanted and what you knew to be true about your life.

Somewhere, all of us, men, women, old, young, black, brown, yellow, white, we forget that moment of our greatness. It gets buried sometimes under the pain of disappointment or failure. When something doesn't work out, like a job, a friendship, a house or a relationship we immediately debit our love-for –self account and enter the debited amount as credit for 'failure'. Over time, every situation that doesn't pan or a challenge, we define as a mistake or a flub up and for some reason, we blame ourselves. This reinforces the notion that we need outside affirmation (success, friendships, money) to continue to grow. This keeps us in a place where we only make decisions that are safe.

Perception

Not that we are not responsible for choices, because we are. We are women and women are responsible for their lives and for their choices. This is not about masking lessons under the 'I love me' banner, but it's more about understanding life as a love-of- self process where you live, learn and grow. I remember watching my niece, who I was raising, in gymnastics class walking on the balance beam and her expressions of fear, joy, exhilaration and trepidation at what she was doing and I thought to myself, "life for us (women) is like that, a balancing act". Sometimes balancing everything and everyone can cause fear, joy, exhilaration, trepidation. It can cause us to feel all of those things and all of those things can bear us down and raise us up, all at once. It is really a matter of perception isn't it? But that perception is the direct result of your experiences. You choose your experiences, whether it is work, school, lovers, family or friends. We choose what kind of experiences we will have and those experiences shape the filter through which we process feelings, thoughts and emotions.

Fear

At one time or another we have all experienced fear, the fleeting kind and the paralyzing kind. Most of us would agree that it is not a state we prefer to live in, and definitely not a state to make decisions in; but many of us still do. We fear being poor, so we hoard. We fear rejection so we tolerate toxic conversation and friendships. We fear being alone so we stay in unsatisfying relationships. Call it social convention, cultural expectations or personal training, we often make decisions based on the fear of what could happen (I will end up broke and alone; I will never find my soul mate; with the recession, I can't start a business) and not the reality. Since the reality is not everyone is going to end up alone, broke or a failure. When we think, we plan, when we plan, we act and when we act, that act becomes a lifestyle. The more you live without fear, the more your lifestyle changes. You become more assertive and successful in business, writing, finances and friendships. You also became healthier physically and psychologically. Your life becomes clearer; you see your goals as your reality.

Agree to make no decision based on fear. If something is uncomfortable, go with it until you are sure that it is no good for you. Sometimes what is uncomfortable is the unknown. The unknown can be good or bad for us. How can we be sure? We can't, that is why it's the unknown, but what we should not do is fill ourselves with anxiety about a future we don't know or control and live today, the good, bad or indifferent. Someone told me that a good life is really about perception. Every day we decide how to see our

Mind, Body, Spirit In Business (Trademark Pending/Copyright Protected,10/21/ 2015)

reality. We live in what we decide. It's a decision; that is what separates us from the animal kingdom, we don't have to live based on fight or flight, impulse driven behavior to achieve the basics in life: food, shelter, safety, sex, etc. We act like every unpleasant or uncomfortable experience is the beginning of the end but it isn't. It really is just the beginning. Live in it. It won't kill you to wait out the uncomfortable.

Ego

Love is a healthy aspect in business as well. Ego and fear infringe into your business as what we call power. Ego is fueled by power and recognition. Yes, you know the law and you won't exercise some things but you will operate outside of your passion to help others. It's wrong!

Altered love can obstruct your view of food, your body and your relationships! That is why it is very important that we look deep within to free those crippling thoughts and ideas.

Creativity Connectors

As women we pride ourselves on our ability to multitask and be independent. We can do most things alone and don't necessarily seek help in supporting our vision and enhancing our goals and accomplishments. Or for support we often stick with a comfortable circle of women based on common interest (work, church, family, etc.). One of the most enriching choices to make is to include in your sister circle women that may be different than you. We call these circles your "Creativity Connectors". Sometimes the most important revelations come from a source that sparks your creativity in a new way or in a way you never experienced. Open your heart to attract and embrace those creativity connectors that can spark a new thought or idea. Some of us were raised to believe that "birds of a feather flock together" or "Iron sharpens Iron" or "be equally yoked", all of these admonishments refer to the importance of connected on a daily basis with individuals that care for you, support your ideals and live according to your shared moral compass. That is one way to looking at it. But perhaps the other way of interpreting these concepts is to see that being "equally yoked" means having similar contentment and life concept.

We would not recommend that you connect creatively with someone detrimental to your health but rather, see friendship and sisterhood as a diverse field of creative opportunity. Trust your inner voice. You know when you meet someone if your creative spirit connects with that person. Our recommendation is to follow that connection, no matter what you were taught to think about them or the type of person they are. For example, many creative women I know are in same sex relationships, they are lesbian. My church circle in some ways forbids intimate socializing with these women but for me, some of my most creative connections are with some gay women. I believe my creative connection overrides their relationship orientation and mine. I also have great spiritual connection with practitioners of spiritual Catholicism and other ancient traditional ritual based religious paths. Connecting with these individuals, priests, nuns, lay practitioners, sparks something in me. When I kneel before the statue of Mother

Mary at the Cenacle retreat house, I feel a creative spark, something resonates within me with her image of feminine divinity and sacredness. Follow Your spark. Embrace it.

<u>A healthy mind</u> is the key to a healthy life.

<u>Fill your mind</u> with peace and good feelings and your mind will give that experience in return. Whatever you are experiencing in your mind now is what you put there earlier on. **Thoughts are powerful.**

Keep your mind filled with positive thoughts. Remember that thoughts and words become things. Choose your words carefully and be mindful of your thoughts. Replace all negative words with positive ones.

Thoughts are like seeds
When you sow a thought you reap an action, when you sow an action you reap a habit, when you sow a habit you reap a character and when you sow a character you reap a destiny. Thoughts are like seeds. You cannot sow the seed of one plant and get another: thistles will never produce daffodils! When your thoughts are positive, powerful and constructive, your life will reflect this.

Think in the right way
Everything depends on your thinking. If you think in the right way you will be light. If you think in a wasteful way you will be heavy. Wasted thoughts are dangerous. They waste your time. They allow the past to come alive, and then you forget the present and question the future.

13

Positive thinking

Positive thinking and optimistic outlook will never produce bad results. Negative thinking and pessimistic approach will never produce good results. Positive thinkers will never fail. Negative thinkers will never succeed.

Creation of the Thinker

Acts of virtue emerge from deep within, from an inner sanctuary of silence from which inspiration flows. Every action has its seed in a thought and every thought is a creation of the thinker, the soul. You choose what thoughts you want to create and as is your thinking so are your actions and also your experience in life. Going within, you touch the stillness and pure love that lie at the core of your being and every thought that you create is of benefit to yourself and of benefit to humanity.

Body

The human body is a very complex mass made up of a Digestive System, Nervous System, Cardiovascular System and Musculoskeletal System.

The Digestive System are organs that help the body break down and absorb food. Parts of the nervous and circulatory systems also play major roles in the digestive system. When we eat food it is not in a form that can be used as nourishment. It has to be broken down into smaller molecules before it is able to be carried to cells throughout our body. Once they are broken down the body is then able to use them to nourish cells and provide energy.

The Nervous System is the information center for the body. Its function is to gather information about the body, analyze it and initiate the appropriate responses to satisfy certain needs. Survival being the most important need. There are several systems of nerves. The brain and the nerves make up the central nervous system, the system responsible for body functions not under our conscious control, such as the heartbeat and digestive system, is the peripheral nervous system. The nervous system uses impulses and as these impulses travel along the cells the information is processed and initiates an action.

The Cardiovascular System includes the heart and the blood vessels, and the respiratory system contains those organs which are responsible for carrying oxygen from the air to the blood stream and expelling the waste product of carbon dioxide. Blood circulates through our bodies, the heart pumps the oxygen into the blood and collects the carbon dioxide which is then expelled out of the body through the lungs. The lungs play a major role in this, but every living cell in the body is involved in the process.

The Musculoskeletal System muscle is attached to the bones and tissue. When muscles move they provide us with a variety of actions by becoming longer or shorter. Muscles are made up of millions of tiny protein filaments which work together to produce motion in the body. Skeletal muscles carry out voluntary movements and these are the muscles that ache after strenuous exercise. Cardiac muscles are those that are found only in the heart and power the action that pumps the blood through our bodies.

Next is Dairy:
Cheese, milk, yogurt. Have 1-2 servings a day.
Next is nuts, seeds, beans and tofu along with fish, poultry and eggs.
Then we have vegetables and fruits, healthy fats and oils (olive, canola, soy, corn, sunflower, peanut), and whole grains (brown rice, whole wheat pasta and oats).

First, Start with Exercise
The base for a healthy diet begins with exercise.
Exercise keeps calories in balance and your weight in check.

Second, focus on the food you eat
Focus on the food and not the grams. The Healthy Eating Pyramid doesn't worry about specific servings or grams of food, so neither should you.

Always Go with Plants

The healthiest diet is a plant based diet. Include plenty of vegetables, fruits, healthy fats and whole grains. Vegetables help reduce the risk of heart disease and strokes, lower blood pressure, lower of the risk of eye and digestive problems and they have a great effect on the blood sugar which can help keep your appetite in check. Your goal should be about 4 1/2 cups of vegetables and fruits a day. Focus on variety and color. Dark leafy green vegetables are the best, don't forget tomatoes and make sure to get yellow, orange and red colors into the diet. Variety is just as important as the quantity.

Don't hide the fruits. Keep them out where you can see them, this way you are more likely to eat them. For your vegetables eat lots and lots of them. Stir fry them, make salads and don't forget they make good snacks too.

Integrate Grains

WHOLE GRAINS

And the word <u>WHOLE</u> is the most important part of grains. Whole means they are rich in fiber, they have healthy fat, vitamins and minerals.

Sources of Whole Grains are:

- Whole wheat berries, whole wheat bulgur, whole wheat couscous and other strains of wheat such as kamut and spelt
- Brown rice (including quick-cooking brown rice)
- Corn, whole cornmeal, popcorn
- Oat groats, steel-cut oats, rolled oats (including quick cooking and instant oatmeal)
- Whole rye

- Hulled barley (pot, scotch, and pearled barley often have much of their bran removed)
- Triticale (pronounced tri-ti-kay-lee)
- Millet
- Teff (reported to be the world's smallest grain and to have a sweet, malt-like flavor)
- Buckwheat, quinoa (pronounced keen-wah), wild rice, and amaranth are considered whole grains even though botanically they are not in the grain family of plants.

If we tried to keep track of all of the vitamins and what they are good for it would be a full time job. So use a multi-vitamin and add some extra vitamin D. This is a great way to insure that you are getting all the nutrients you need to be healthy. And please avoid megadoses of vitamins!

Healing the Immune System

A full eight hours of sleep a night is the best way to heal the immune system. While sleeping your body will heal the immune system. So be sure and get eight hours of sleep per night. And this needs to be eight straight, uninterrupted hours of sleep. Keeping your immune system healthy is the best way to avoid illnesses. Keep healthy. Eat the correct foods, take your vitamins, get exercise, drink plenty of fluids (especially water) and get a good eight hours of sleep per night.

Choices

E-EMOTIONS. .

Eating - E

Every choice we make should be calculated and measured. Consider the options and possible outcomes to each element of the choice: financial, mental and emotional, before making a decision. Especially when it is work related since work plays an important role in our critical growth time.

Exercise - E

Choices are conscious and we choose our path and the direction to take. Even consequences of our paths are a choice since most times we are aware of the results of our choices, good or bad or indifferent. Our current reality is a choice too. How we live today is a direct result of choices we make historically.

Some choices are decisions that you make impetuously and some are what you spend months, maybe years considering. There are few types of choices, some are critical and some are mundane. No matter the type you must dedicate your attention to them.

Moments - M

Take moments in the morning or evening and plan to pack 5 vegetables for your day plan. Put it in the car when you wake up or pack it in your bag the night before.

Work: Is your job killing you?

We spend between 40-80 hours a week at and preparing for work. There are only 120 hours of time in the work week of 5 days of 24 hours each. So that means we spend 1/3 or sometimes half of that time preparing for or being at work. Now what I am about to suggest is absolutely radical and may even be scary for you and that suggestion is to think long and hard about your work choices. It took me a major surgery and a series of major anxiety attacks to realize that 9 to 5 work in an office atmosphere was killing me. Not that you should not work or should you try to avoid work, but rather you must consider the type of work and the work environment you choose for yourself. I have a great friend from the PhD program that clocks 100 hours a week; has a set of twins and lives out of a suitcase traveling the world for a major pharmaceutical company and she is happy. Plus she makes over $200,000 a year! Not bad for a sister the north side of fifty recently divorced. It works for her! Go for it girl! I celebrate and support her.

But for many of us that are not compensated anywhere near the level we need to be happy and prosperous, working in jobs out of necessity, work is often toil not triumph. Becoming an entrepreneur is for many of us, a multi-year odyssey. This is something you really must think through. Entrepreneurship is one of the only career options you have to really control your time, energy, resources and destiny. Work is too critical of a function in our lives in America to think you can just "do whatever you have to do". The Great Recession taught us that even when you follow all the rules and "do what you have to do", it is still not enough, and you can still end up broke, disillusioned and unemployed.

Therefore, you must consider all possibilities to support your workplace choice satisfaction. Some folks can work in a government environment where sometimes the most important thing is coming to work on time and leaving on time; punching in and out. Some of us can work in a solely independent work environment as an entrepreneur where you set the rules, time and resources limits.

Your mental, physical and emotional health is impacted by your work environment. Heart, kidney and lung disease are all impacted by your work type and environment. How many people do we know with debilitating supposed manageable diseases working a 9 to 5 in an office for less than $100,000? Now, how many people do we know with debilitating supposed manageable diseases working as a full time entrepreneur making less than $100,000? I don't know many since ...

The truth is that most successful entrepreneurs are healthy and happy! Not just because of the limitless earning potential but in my many talks with successful business owners, the joy they get from controlling and managing their own time, energy and resources contributes to overwhelming contentment which often manifests itself as optimal mental, emotional and physical health.

Yes, you can spend 40 to 80 hours a week doing things you hate in a place you can't stand and still retire good, but the energy required to do that robs you of other important things like good sleep, a healthy weight, spiritual purity and clarity of mind - all things you need to plan your retirement and enjoy it to the fullest. For some, the spector of a pension is that important that working in a toxic environment for 10 or 20 years is worth it, but to make the retirement worth it and enjoyable they must be diligent and savvy enough to balance the toxicity with enough positive clear thinking. As one person put it, you must have a "prosperity mindset" and be able to clearly determine and believe that there is no scarcity in your life and that no matter where you find yourself – even in a toxic work environment – you will have the best in health, clarity and spiritual purity.

Again, it is all in the choices you make. Only you can decide if your job is killing you and your potential and your goals. Then you have to make a choice based on that decision.

The Pursuit of Happiness

Change never results in failure. Change is always a victory. Change can be perceived as failure but the reality is our perception is informed by those around us and our environment so if you socialize with fearful insecure people, your perception of change will be fear-inducing. Working with individuals whose lives are ruled by fear is also crippling. Their fear, their insecurities are projected in their behavior toward others. A desire for power, purpose, and importance makes them toxic, controlling and provocative in their behavior. These types of people are not really satisfied until they get a rise out of someone. They have to have reaction, usually of the negative variety. All of us have fallen victim to this type of person since it challenges or goes against what we believe to be right or fair. The truth of the matter is these types of individuals cannot be reached without mental health intervention. So we have a choice to make: fight an unbeatable battle or choose our own soft landing. This could mean leaving a job with steady income, staying in a relationship and working things out or leaving. It could mean rethinking your life strategy. When life's roads get rocky, sometimes it's best to change paths.

Health and Wealth?

How can we increase our health and our wealth? In meeting with millionaires around the world, famed author Keith Cameron said that one of the most enduring qualities of all the millionaires he spoke to said that they were happy, filled with joy and this in turn enhanced their overall health. They did not express fear about health. It is amazing how people with less means are often most plagued by medical issues. Health is absolutely influenced by exposure and resources but what about those folks in different parts of the world that lack resources but are joyfully living their vision and are healthy?

There must be a connection between health and our belief system and having wealth. Wealth is expressed physically, spiritually and emotionally. Jesus, the Christ, was one of the most spiritually and emotionally wealthy and healthy people to walk the earth. We can all agree to that! What was so wealthy and healthy about Jesus? **His mind. His entire way of thinking**. All of his followers had what they needed and what they all wanted more of was Jesus' way of thinking. Each person that adopted Jesus' way of thinking, became more wealthy, healthy and whole. Health and wealth (in all of its manifestations) are bonded, connected eternally. Your health is connected to your wealth. The healthier you become, the wealthier you are. It is your decision every day. Before jumping on that conference call, the computer or telephone first thing in the morning, practice some quiet movement or exercise and eat something healthy. Whenever I hear a woman say that she doesn't eat breakfast or she is not a breakfast person I immediately feel a sense of pain or loss for that person since the first thing in the morning – the first two to three hours – are your most energetically important and sustenance in the morning (no matter how simple) is the trigger to start your healthy journey for the day. The first two hours upon awakening are our most important, remember that. Let no obligation rob you of the first two hours for your health. If you are responsible for waking and preparing small children for school – as I am – wake before them (maybe 40 to 60 minutes) and **take care of your needs first**. Pack lunch the night before, lay out the clothes and give baths all the night before. That way your child's morning routine can be complete within 30 minutes. Also, put the children to bed early. This is a major oversight we often make. In the effort to spend time with our children, we keep them up entirely too late, robbing us of important end-of-day time.

The truth is – we know our bodies and we know when things are not right. We make the choice to be happy or joyful or not. We cannot blame anyone else. *"Seek ye first the kingdom of heaven"*, we hear this scripture a lot, most times out of context! What is the Kingdom of Heaven if not starting with your heart? **How can you contemplate, embrace or consider the heavenly realms when you heart and your body and mind are out of balance**?

Where does your energy go?

Energy is life force, it is spirit. That is the substance of what we see and experience but can only experience through all of our senses. Energy is required for all things – movement, growth, progression, change. The sun is the single most important energy source for our planet providing vitamins, purifying and illumination. Your energy level is paramount for your life to be fruitful. The sun provides the nutrient trigger so that plant life can photosynthesize. The same is true of our lives. We need energy to photosynthesize, that is to take in oxygen (the breath of life) to trigger a chain reaction that will both restore our being and produce offspring or outcome to share with our connected family. It is a chain reaction. Your energy is used internally for your optimal operationalization with enough to then share as an outcome with others. **Often times we use our already depleted energy levels to "help" others instead of using our energy to restore, rejuvenate and grow ourselves so that we can "share" our offspring or outcome with others**. We confuse giving energy away with sharing our energy surplus.

Helping vs. Sharing

Many of us were taught, and had it reinforced, that we as women were designed to be a "helpmate". This definition was based on the biblical reference that Eve, the mother of human creation, was only designed to provide a role to her husband Adam to help. But what if her role as mother (creative feminine divine) was to share her energy with Adam, the animals, the plants, the earth and so forth? In other words, perhaps her role was to share with the earth her divine energy, the feminine life force that permeates all living things. It is all in your perspective and self-talk. Without Eve, none of Adam's pursuits would have been completed. If you subscribe to the Judeo-Christian explanation for the first two human inhabitants of the earth, you can believe it more fully when you embrace a new concept of your energy as surplus life force that can be shared so that you call allow others to help themselves. Energy is life-force and that energy is directed by thoughts, words and actions.

Make the Connection

Exercise:

1. Make the first 10 minutes of the day movement. Get out of bed, touch your toes, stretch your back and breathe. Say simply: Today all is well. I am happy.

2. Say one of affirmations out loud on the CD in your car.

3. Write here what exercise you can do each day for 10 minutes (jumping jacks, three yoga poses, walk your hallway 5 times) that gets your heart pumping before you leave your bedroom.

'Innercise':

1. Every time a negative thought or word enters your mind, say out loud it's complete opposite! Instead of running to the meeting saying, "I'm going to show them who's boss!" Say, "I am going to show them a humble and happy servant leader".

Write hear two positive remarks you can say everyday out loud to someone else that you would like to hear every day:

Spirit

Questions from within – Edna's Story

Friday February 2007 the day that I finally acknowledged my questions, out loud, and the first lock was opened. I saw that those bully prayers went to the ceiling and bounced back down, because the words were not reality but someone else's wish. I had to listen to my intuition and learn on my own because I dare not question another human being who was ordained set aside for the purpose of directing someone else like me. I would question myself over and over, however I was really questioning the spirit that was God inside me. Which was right? For decades I had kept silent and remained repeating the same religious practices again again with no action proof or abundance. God was speaking and I was too programmed to hear.

When you hear questions coming from inside you, that's your intuition speaking. Listen.

I am sure that those reading this book today have gotten to a point they now realize persons demanding anyone to "shouldn't, couldn't, wouldn't and your better not" are the persons they are not to render their minds, bodies or business to. If God gives us free will and trusts us to make mistakes, how can a mere human suggest otherwise? I'm not saying to not abide by laws, rules or regulations which don't require your emotions to follow, but when it dictates how you emotionally bond with, emotionally move and directly progress in your life, those choices to follow must be re-evaluated. Being who you are and knowing who you are, sets those limits or makes you limitless. Many of us forget the church was originally for the law and the lost. A reminding place where you are reminded of your values and to direct the knowledge you have what it takes to make this journey. Pretty neat trick, to use your willpower, choice!

Spirituality or consciousness or divine intent is a meaningful practice individually understood and personally implemented as a means of finding and connecting to the divine self, it's a private journey. Spiritual purity on the other hand is another step to finding the divine self. Being spiritually pure means knowing, understanding and implementing in your life, real actions that support your spiritual journey. What we mean is **how good is spirituality for you if you don't or can't translate it to the choices you make? That is the key**. We can all have a spiritual identity, spiritual path, or religious tradition but how good is it for you if you can't depend on it to guide you in ways that strengthen or improve your state or place in this life? Spirituality is eternally transcendent but grounded in your real life today. It is two-fold: belief and action. Understanding and progression.

For those of us that have had the experience of divorce, this is even more potent a reminder to learn from our past since all marriages are a two-way road, there is a part we all play. Not that there are not instances where abuse and utter disregard by a party forces the other to leave, but in most cases we can remove the rose-colored lenses and admit to ourselves the role we played or did not play in the death of a marital or intimate relationship. Spiritual purity is a commitment that we make to ensure that our spiritual choices and practices lead us to supportive, positive choices: leaving when it's time and staying when its right in any situation be it friendship, lovers, family or work.

The universe is made of small particles naked to the eye. These particles combine with other particles and create patterns, readable shapes and contours in outer space that impact our lives here on earth in weather patterns, temperature, food, animals and life. Based on what we see in the universe informs what we believe to be true about the world around us: religion, family, love, money, friendships, etc.

Our spiritual purity is like the universe, influenced by millions of small things: actions, experiences, disappointments, enjoyment, etc. These small particles combine to create a path, a shape, a contour of who we are and our place in the world. This path leads our life, our choices and our experiences. Spiritual Purity is simple: do you honor what your path teaches you? The principles you learn in and from should reinforce your decision making and the choices you make.

Satisfied: Being content is about more than having what you want.

You can be satisfied without having everything you want. It is true that satisfaction is often hard to find and difficult to maintain. We equate being satisfied with having the right mix of things in our lives but you can be satisfied without having everything you want in your life. Contentment is a natural outgrowth of being satisfied. Being satisfied is accomplishing or achieving your mission or purpose in life. Being content is the emotional attachment you have to being satisfied, it is embracing your life, it is a feeling of wellness, positivity and clarity about what you have in your life today.

See, we can be satisfied without ever being truly content. Look at the person who has accomplished all of their emotional and professional goals yet feels uneasy or incomplete about their choices. They are not content. Contentment is long-term satisfaction. When you are content you have a feeling of power and positivity that radiates from within and it impacts others around you, your family, your co-workers, your lover, spouse, friends and neighbors.

The process of becoming satisfied starts very early in life. **Just like someone battling food addiction , learning your triggers for overeating, knowing when you are full, planning meals, are all ways people learn how to be satisfied with healthy eating instead food addiction**. It is the same with our lives; we learn early on whether or not to be and how to be satisfied with events, people, experiences, etc. This same process for satisfaction translates into our personal lives as well. How do we determine satisfaction? How is it measured in your life? These are questions to ponder since each of us has a different life satiation level or rate. Some of us can take satisfaction in the small victories, like working out in the morning or keeping the gas tank above half a tank while others of us, only feel satisfied in accomplishing the big things in life like getting a new job or finishing school. The truth is we learn to be content more when we have a basic satiation rate with life; when we can take satisfaction in the small things in life.

Scaling down to build up

Doing the opposite of what seems natural can often yield the best results. How so? Forgive when wronged; give instead of take. Create versus destroy. We see time and again in our lives how doing the opposite can net positive long-term results in our lives. Trust versus being suspicious; love instead of fear. We are often weighted down by societal expectations and use those societal expectations to make decisions in our lives. Lose weight, build muscle.

Free

Thoughts, behavior, consequences and relationships can cause us to be free or they can weigh us down. Real freedom is living authentically. There is nothing more heavy or burdensome then living a life that is not yours or a vision that you did not create. We try to convince ourselves that we do things because that is what a relationship, marriage or love requires. But if those things are in direct opposition to who you really are and what makes you content (remember the difference between contentment and happiness) then how is that freedom?

Many women are taught to believe that love and relationships are "work". Yes, work is required to accomplish goals, to achieve success and to overcome obstacles but the core driving force in your relationship cannot always be work or a struggle. The relationship/love part of an intimate relationship or friendship should be free of manacles and weight. That part should be the most carefree, rewarding and illuminating factor in your life. Relationships where there is constant miscommunication, required redirection and strife begin to take a toll on you emotionally. Sometimes the signs are physical: fatigue, weight gain, snappishness. Or the signs can be emotional: lack of fulfillment emotionally, sexually or physically; a void that cannot be explained or identified. Each of us knows when our planets are out of alignment but the truth is, most of us know within months of a new relationship whether or not the relationship will require a level of effort we cannot or don't want to give.

Soul Ties

Author Danielle Tate writes in her book "Soul Ties" that soul ties are "*A spiritual connection between two people who have been physically intimate with each other **or who have had an intense emotional or spiritual association or relationship**.*"

For the purpose of this discussion we address soul tie from the perspective of an intense emotional or spiritual association or relationship. Friendships, family and business partners can all produce soul ties, but we must be careful about labeling experiences as a "tie". Some experiences although long lasting in their impact may not be a tie that must be broken and/or removed. Some soul ties are important and fruitful, like those in your primary love relationship or sisterhood circles. These spiritual connections are valuable to you as you creatively connect and continue to renew and deepen your commitment to the divine femininity within. Trusting your choices and decisions to the Universe (God, The Divine Beloved, All There is) is like sunshine and water to the soul tie seeds you have planted. Therefore, be fully present and emotionally attuned to the spiritual connections you make with people in church, school, work, home and community since your life force (energy) will bond with them creating a cyclical connection. For example if you have a friendship where you have changed or developed in another way, thereby reducing your commonality, you may still be connected to that persons emotional cycles and automatically respond to their changes. There was a time when I drank socially in an over-moderate way with a certain circle of people. We each knew when we were going to "tie one on" based on certain experiences during our time apart be it stress at work, church, community, etc. We intuitively knew – even without seeing each other or being around each other– when to call and set up a time to "belly-up" together at the nearby watering hole. We had a soul tie that included over moderate drinking. Over time, we each developed and changed in a way where that deep emotional and spiritual connection to alcohol indulgence waned, faded and then fell away completely. Think about your soul ties, the ones you want to enhance and those to release. Are there intense spiritual and emotional connections that you want to multiply in your life and learn more from?

Financial Bondage

Beyond simply passing the collection plate every Sunday, many churches did not rightfully teach about personal finance. Yes you were told to have insurance and pay tithes but that is as far as it went. I know I was tired of living in (financial) crisis yet I looked for that support where I felt safe and I still did not obtain that goal. I set out on my own to teach myself first then show my children how it can work. I want to share here the symptoms of financial bondage, then you can ask yourself, "Am I in financial bondage?" Financial bondage exists when there is excessive debt or a preoccupation with wealth or misuse of it. The most common type of financial bondage is the excessive use of credit. Many people think they'll not be allowed to borrow more than they can afford to pay. This simply isn't true! On top of this, creditors are allowed to charge even more interest on delinquent accounts. It's simply a no-win situation.

Symptoms of Bondage

Overdue bills stemming from the lack of planning and from overspending.

Investment Worries - worrying about your financial assets is bondage. If your investments cause worry, you can be sure you're not in God's will. Matthew 6:24-25 tells us that we cannot serve both God and money, and that life is more important than things.

Get-Rich-Quick Attitude - the tell-tale signs here are taking on excessive debt, borrowing money to invest, or dealing deceitfully with people. Always assess your true motives for financial involvement.

No Gainful Employment - the expectation is that those who work should support those who don't. This is wrong! Another instance of entitlement. Naturally, this does not include circumstances involving a prolonged illness or a legitimate disability. But when it involves able-bodied people, this form of financial bondage is selfishness to the core!

Deceit - being dishonest in financial matters will strip away peace and contentment. An obvious example is lying about what something is worth. But think about it: Purchasing something on credit when you know you're already behind on your bills falls into this category too. Luke 16:10 reminds us that "whoever can be trusted with very little can also be trusted with much, and whoever is dishonest with very little will also be dishonest with much."

Greed - this is what underlies always wanting the best, or always wanting more. Not being able to put others' needs first, never able to accept a necessary loss, or always looking at what others have = Greed. We must learn to put our *wants* aside in order to satisfy the *needs* of others in order to avoid this financial bondage trap.

Coveting - wanting what others have. This attitude, especially among the young, is all too easy to slip into, and starts the downhill spiral to financial bondage. Peace and contentment should be our goals.

Unmet Family Needs - this is usually a by-product of one or many of those issues already mentioned. And, unless such circumstances are due to illness, injury, or unforeseen events, it all boils down to irresponsibility. Plain and simple.

Lack of Charity - we are called to help supply the needs of those who cannot do so for themselves. To refuse to do so in a tangible way is selfish and short-sighted.

Over commitment to Work - devotion to business pursuits that excludes all else is bondage. We are called to *excellence*, not over-commitment. Know the difference.

Money Entanglements - these stem from mishandling finances, perhaps even deceitfully. Entanglements require continual manipulation to keep the mess from collapsing.

Financial Unfairness - this involves promoting our own interests to the detriment of others. High-pressure sales tactics can fall into this category, especially when used in dealing with recent widows or others under duress. Taking advantage of a situation or a relationship, rather than focusing on the value of what is offered, is deceptive and selfish.

Financial Superiority - this occurs in those blessed with abundance. Wealth is not an honor or a right, but a responsibility. Those who have much should share it with those who have little, and do it without demanding attention. In the last days, there will be no provision for the financially superior. We will all be equal and it's that is to those who have planned accordingly.

Financial Resentment - this attitude comes from the mindset that are entitled and we should have what we deserve or desire. We covet what others have and are resentful toward our station in life. One quick attitude-check is to remember how most of the rest of the world lives --- even our pets eat better than they do!

Financial bondage can grow out of any of four conditions:

• a lack of money

• overspending

• an abundance of money

• a misunderstanding of how money is to be used.

Continuing to adjust our spending level to exceed our income will result in financial bondage. Borrowing is the most common pathway into bondage.

Coming back from these states is a simple switch of contentment. Contentment does not come from having what you want, but from realizing how much you already have. When we are satisfied with what we have, we are content. This is true wealth.

Contentment does not come from riches

• it can never be found in material possessions

• it does not come when things get better

• contentment is not complacency: it is not *resigning yourself* to your situation

• it does not change when your circumstances change

Contentment is intrinsic, not extrinsic. It is an attitude, a frame of mind, that does not depend on external circumstances

• it is feeling secure and at peace

• it is satisfaction and acceptance of our circumstances

• it is a daily decision of gratitude and trust

• it is counting even the little things as blessings

• it is keeping your joy

• contentment is learned

As you can see, money and contentment do not go hand-in-hand. *Stop and think about how much you already have to be grateful for.*

Remember....

#1 There are things much <u>more important than money</u>: character, integrity, a good reputation, good relationships, wisdom, etc.

#2 There are things money cannot buy: true friends, peace, and salvation.

#3 We must answer the question What Is Success? in order to be content.

First and foremost, success is a lack of bondage. Second, success is having the ability to be involved in the things that really matter the most in life. *But ultimately, the secret to contentment is a balanced life.*

The Connection – Nicole's Story

Getting on track...

So you have your goals worked out and know your calling and in your mind's eye you know what you would be doing if money, time and restrictions had no bearing. You talk, you plan, you strategize, you partner but it doesn't provide the outcome you are seeking. Why isn't it happening for you? Enslavement and fear are what we call "twin tie-downs" and they often take different forms in your life: constant fatigue, weight gain, mindless eating, feelings of emptiness, insomnia, weak immunity, anxiety, lack of sex drive or no interest in anything sensual since you are too tired or depressed about your body, image or any other issue. These 'dis-eases' are your body's tune fork that vibrates at levels that will more likely grab your attention. Weight did it for me. When I pushed the scales at 226 pounds at 5'9 and 36 years old my doctor told me you have five strikes against you: (1) you are African American; (2) you are over 35; (3) you are overweight; (4) you have diabetes in your family; (5) you are female. My doctor told me that if I did not lose at least 20% of my body weight (40 pounds) then I would surely become diabetic and develop hypertension. I remember driving to Ruby Tuesday to get a drink and I passed World Gym and the sign said "$99 Summer Special". I had just got paid and had to pay cable that day and get gas. I went in and the manager there told me that if I joined that day – July 1, she would take $50 now and then another $50 at the end of the month.

Mind, Body, Spirit In Business (Trademark Pending/Copyright Protected, 2015)

I joined that day and took Zumba the next morning. I never looked back – now 50 pounds later I can say that I literally owe my life to World Gym since I was on a ride that would have led me to sure hospitalization. I do not allow any obligation to take precedent over my healthy eating or workouts. They are non-negotiable. I travel on the road in my car about 3 hours a day and often work in 2 to 3 different sites so I carry a bag of food for the day: a smoothie, a protein drink, 3 fruit, a bag of nuts or a granola bar, lunch (usually a salad) and a dinner (usually a can of soup or a refrigerated salad or sandwich). I do not leave eating to chance or convenience. I also reduced stress within my control in all areas of my life for the first year including marriage relationship, 9 to 5 work, church obligation and community volunteerism. I lost 30 pounds the first year and 10 pounds a year each year after that. I am now a healthy size 12/14 down from my unhealthy 18/20. Maybe your body vibration will send you signal through migraines, sleeplessness, snappishness, or overall malaise.

Family: Victim or Villain?

Every family is almost like a play where every member is assigned a role or has one designed for them. It has been observed that some families have cast members into two distinct roles: victim or villain. Either you are a victim, someone that is consistently abused, mistreated, or otherwise disregarded or you are a villain. This is the person painted as the most worrisome, unruly or uncontrollable or most misunderstood and/or maligned. It is often the case that when a member of the "cast" decides to forgo, reprise or abandon their role all together, the rest of the cast either alienates them or stages some sort of intervention or family showdown where the errant actor is "pulled back into the fold". Some families work best when everyone's behavior is "acceptable" or "predictable". If or when you decide to deviate from your clan's acceptable traditions, roles, behavior, language and choices, you must be prepared to accept the outcome. You may be alienated, cast from the group or imitated as a role model. No matter if you are a victim or villain, understand you play a role in every interpersonal relationship you have – either to your betterment or your detriment. I hear women justify or explain to me all the time the reasons why they are not making their self-care a priority – they don't have the time, money, support or resources.

I have come to the conclusion, even in my own life that the roles we agree to play in our families carry over into all other areas of life. So if you were not taught, shown and had it reinforced that your healthy eating, sleeping, exercise and self care were a priority for your overall success, then how in the world could you possibly apply those principles now? Take a moment and write down the role you think you played growing up, victim, villain or some other role. Do you play that role now emotionally? In other words, do you return to those same emotions now in your life like a bedrock? For example if you were the victim, the person who absorbed blame for things, when you experience an emotional situation, do you return to feeling like a victim and acting like one? Think about your responses. I used to be a very impulsive confronter. If I heard, saw or experienced something I did not like, I immediately moved to confront you – verbally and often times profanely. I was not a person that tolerated any slight. I had been programmed in my childhood through family dynamics and situations to not "let anybody treat me like no fool". So I set out each day to make sure that no one played me like an all-day sucker. I was hyper vigilant and my cortisol and estrogen levels reflected it. Clearly my confrontational style was not benefiting me and my life force reflected this reality. I am still growing into the woman that I experience in my sister circle: patient, encouraging, funny, loving and open. Think about your role and how it impacts your thinking, feeling and decision making. No one will be perfect but we can all live perfectly as true selves! Forget the roles and follow your inner voice that leads and guides you to the elements of true joy for you.

Honor your SPIRIT

We are first and foremost "*spiritual*" beings.

Growing Spiritually

It's not easy to grow spiritually in today's modern world, where everything seems to boil down to money, power and influence.

Over the last decade more and more we have focused our attention on physical needs and wants. **Extensively helped by our society, the media, television, magazines and the World Wide Web, we have learned to chase external rewards, instead of seeking a balance between the material and spiritual aspects of our lives**. We have allowed ourselves to be distracted by the various pictures of success that society offers us. We constantly compare ourselves with others and we are living according to someone else's idea of what life should be. So, large amounts of people have lost control of their lives and vast groups of them live a confused and unhappy life, while others are in different states of depression.

If the self-motivation tips we provide are followed you will start to live a more balanced spiritual life. Self-motivation exercises help us to grow into the balanced spiritual person we want to be.

To be able to grow spiritually we need to look inside of ourselves, this goes beyond recalling certain events that took place today, this week or the past month.

We need to learn to be courageous and willing to find the truths that lie deep within us. Introspection means that we have to look closely and reflect on our thoughts and feelings, our beliefs and our motivations in an objective and self-forgiving way and we need to focus on our areas that need improvement. It is important that we periodically examine our experiences, our relationships, the decisions we take, the things that we attract into our lives.

This provides us with deep insights on what our motivations for certain actions are. It gives us the opportunity to look at the qualities of character we want to sustain and the ones we need to adjust or even change, so that we learn to properly act, react and conduct in any situation in our lives.

Growing spiritually means we learn to be able to live our full potential and we need to make sure that our physical body, our mental body, our emotional body and our spiritual body are in balance. Achieving to bring balance to each of these bodies will lead to our total development. Growing spiritually also means that we realize that our lives have a purpose and that we are connected to all things. Our purpose puts all our physical, mental, emotional and spiritual potentials into use. It sustains us during challenging times and it gives us a feeling of having a goal to achieve, a destination to reach. After all we all need a purpose, a meaning. Realizing that we are connected to all things helps us to become more humble and respectful of the people and all things in nature. It makes us appreciative to everything around us and it helps us to go beyond our comfort zone and reach out to others.

To grow in spirit is a day-to-day encounter and the most important thing is that we learn, so that our further spiritual growth is possible.

Nurture your Spirit each and every day.

BODY MIND SPIRIT PAY IT FORWARD

Mind, Body, Spirit In Business (Trademark Pending/Copyright Protected, 2015)

Pay it forward

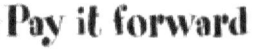

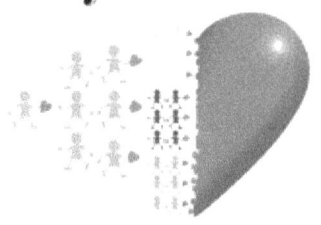

How to Pay It Forward

The world can seem like an unfriendly, threatening place, yet we all want safety, health, and happiness for ourselves and our loved ones. How can one ordinary person -- you or me -- make a positive difference in this world? One way is the practice "paying it forward." While the steps might be simple, the outcome could change the world.

Steps

1. Be attentive wherever you are for opportunities to help someone. Perhaps you have an elderly or disabled neighbor who is too proud to ask for help with their yard work; or maybe you're in a restaurant and see someone who looks like they could use some kind stranger to pay for their meal. You can change people's attitudes about the world through your unobtrusive acts of kindness.
2. Do something nice for someone you don't know (or don't know very well). It should be something significant, and not for a person from whom you expect a good deed -- or anything at all, for that matter -- in return.
3. Spread the word. If the person thanks you and wants to "repay" you (that is, pay it "back"), let them know that what you'd really like is for them to pay it

"forward" -- you'd like them to do something nice for three people they don't know, and ask those three people to do something nice for three more people. The idea is to consciously increase the goodness of the world.

4. Pay it forward. When you notice that somebody has done something nice for you, make a note in your mind to practice three acts of kindness towards other people, as described in Step 2.

****_BONUS*_**

IF YOU WERE "LAID OFF" (OUR DEFINITION IS THAT YOU WERE "FREED") DURING THE GLOBAL FINANCIAL CRISIS (GFC), THEN YOU MUST BE SURE TO CLEANSE YOUR MIND, BODY AND SPIRIT OF THE RESIDUAL ENERGY OF FEAR, SCARCITY, FAILURE AND REJECTION.

Three things you should know before your next job/career/path search

First, speak aloud

AFFIRMATIONS FOR THOSE PERSONALLY AFFECTED BY THE GFC OF 2007-2010:

1. I AM RENEWED

2. MY NEW VISION OF LIFE IS FULL OF FINANCIAL REWARD, SPIRITUAL NOURISHMENT AND MORE THAN ENOUGH TO SHARE WITH OTHERS.

3. I AM WISE

4. I TRUST THE UNIVERSE TO GUIDE ME TO MY PROMISE

Second, acknowledge the anxiety and fear produced by the Global Financial Crisis.

1. **_The recession will not end in (Y)our lifetime._**

   There were so many purported causes of the recession. I can't keep count. It was the housing market, it was military spending, it was weapons of mass destruction. After reading five or six books and watching five documentaries about it, I gave up trying to untangle the mangled threads leading to the beginning of this mess. What I did know was that based on casual observation, the impact of the recession would linger throughout my working life. Seventeen job interviews in less than a year, mentoring relationships going on autopilot. At the end of my thirties, I knew that the next 25 years were the make or break years for me and that I had to land and plant roots in a wealth generating field soon. Face facts, your career path and all of the suppositions your education supported, are forever gone. Billionaire rappers, bankrupt technology companies, pension meltdowns, reality "telelife" are just a few of the contradictions in the life of the Gen X'r. The best thing to do is to face the facts: you will have to change course and chart a new path. Period. Your education, your networking skills and your fancy titles will not get you in the place your parents were at your age. Only a hunger-driven focus on the journey will help you navigate the new wealth landscape.

2. ***Starting your own business is no longer just an option; it's your only means for direction and purpose.***

Everywhere fear abounds. You will get hired, promoted, laid off, terminated, replaced, trained, developed, supported, rejected, abandoned all based on someone else's fear. No decision about you at work will any longer be based solely on your potential, your ability or even your personality. Someone somewhere will be afraid of you or for you. The recession has shaken everyone to the core. Who would ever believe that America could lose its grip on Superpower status? Since fear is the overwhelming foundation for most decision makers it explains why most 70 year old's are still working, why mentoring has dried up and why so many of us on the cusp of our 40's are at loose ends. We just aren't worth the risk anymore. So what do you do? Find an outlet, one that will preferably pay you a salary. Put your degree to work by creating your own job. Thank God I went to a college (Marymount) and grad school (George Mason) that had STRONG entrepreneurial overtones even before it was popular. If you went to a school that worked hard to keep their alumni ahead of the game, class sizes small with professors that had both real-world and professional experience, preferably of the entrepreneurship type, you are in luck! You have the requisite skill to hang out a shingle. Print a business card. Do an inventory of every type of job you've ever had and try to figure out what you did that made you better at it them most people, then zero in on that edge and couple it with a for-profit enterprise. You can be an entrepreneur, you can and will have health insurance and you can and will have more than enough money to retire comfortably if you wish when you are ready. All of the things we think we need a job for, you can actually create yourself.

3. ***Ditch the "Work" crowd.***

Stop hanging around and listening to those that work for others. All they will do is encourage you to continue down a path that is slowly disappearing or that will keep you away from your real potential. Hang out with people that do things you have no depth in. If you were an accountant, hang out with college professors or mystery writers. If you were a lawyer, hang out with tennis coaches or personal trainers. Whatever you did before, ditch that crowd, except for those individuals that really fed your soul and will remain constants in your life no matter what your choices are. The worst thing you can do right now is hang out with people holding on to yesteryear. You need friends and a circle of people that are powerful because of their life choices, not their titles, job, houses, family connections, etc.

Finally, Choose love every time.

It is true; love is the only thing out there now that really is free. We Generation X'er's are hopeless romantics but can be scary-cats when it comes to love and relationships. We started online dating! Hello! But now we really have to face facts, being along all the time isn't always as fun spending time with someone you like being around. So if you have the chance to hang out with someone knew or you got hurt a few times and are considering moving into a monastery; stop burying yourself in an endless pursuit of the next big gig. Find a hand to hold, lips to kiss, a space to be you and a space to make mistakes, demands, express desires. Forget about ten years from now. Focus on being physically healthy and enjoy today.

Without love, there really is nothing else. Love is all we really need. Honestly.

Finding peace, love and living your life is about trusting the voice inside of you; listening to what that voice says and where it directs you. Never doubting that your lifetime of experience can lead you in the right direction.

The Authors

Edna J. White is a supportive & loving coaching resource that promotes sexual abuse prevention to the youth and helps adults process childhood sexual abuse. Edna J. White is passionate about bringing hope, education and motivation to fellow sexual abuse survivors as they work to optimize their lives. She is a former Real Estate Broker and sexual abuse survivor who has transitioned to a career as a Emotional Recovery & Mindset Coach. Ms. White desire is to utilize her personal life experience, past educational background, counseling and coach training to help fellow sexual abuse survivors.

Her background includes 20 years of chapel youth director and public speaking, uniquely qualifies to help fellow survivors get their lives on track faster through better knowledge, empathy and mastery of concrete goals to live the best life possible for them. Visit her website at www.Livingfromtheinsideout.tk

Her show Wounded to Wonderful Talk radio on www.blogtalkradio.com is a gathering place for anyone seeking coaching and real talk about the challenges of life on life's terms. We discuss useful tools that have helped us lighten the load, of our journey through coaching. This is a "we" life coaching program, because it is in the "we," that we find the new "me." We focus on the four A's of Recovery: Awareness, Acceptance, Action and Adaptation. This is a place for survivor's striving to become thrivers.

Nicole Jean Christian, a successful 'Soul-preneaur', award winning grant writer, published author and organizational behavior expert, college professor, doctoral student, affirmation generator, developed the **Mind Body Spirit in Business** philosophy from ten years of research working with hundreds of entrepreneurs from around the world. Nicole has been published and presented in the Journal of Public Affairs Education and over a dozen times in the Conference Proceedings of the Northeast Business and Economic Association and the Conference Proceedings of the Northeast Decision Sciences Institute. Her area of expertise is leadership, organizational behavior and entrepreneurship. Nicole has helped over 100 small businesses and municipal agencies receive over $5 Million dollars in grant funding. She is the creator of ***The Spiritual Entrepreneur***, a trademarked affirmation and mindset process that has changed the lives of thousands. Nicole holds a BBA from Marymount University, a MPA from George Mason University with an advanced certificate in Nonprofit Management. Nicole is also a doctoral student at Walden University. She has been featured in the LIBN's Annual 40/Under 40 Business Leaders to Watch and is a regular guest on 'Domesticology©: The Radio Show', a nationally syndicated radio show on topics such as love, business and success. Nicole is the

Mind, Body, Spirit In Business (Trademark Pending/Copyright Protected, 2015)

resident *Coupling Coach* on the show. All of Nicole's beliefs center on the universal truth that <u>God's love inside of us guides us to all truth.</u> <u>Discover your truth.</u>

<u>Contact us:</u> *We present to support groups, and large groups on over 100 topics such as: Self-Sabotage, Coupling, Creating Peace At Work, and more. .*

www.ingramcontent.com/pod-product-compliance
Lightning Source LLC
Chambersburg PA
CBHW071239220526
45468CB00002B/929